SUMMER AGAIN

David Cregan
SUMMER AGAIN

OBERON BOOKS
LONDON

WWW.OBERONBOOKS.COM

First published in 2004 by Oberon Books Ltd
521 Caledonian Road, London N7 9RH
Tel: +44 (0) 20 7607 3637 / Fax: +44 (0) 20 7607 3629
e-mail: info@oberonbooks.com
www.oberonbooks.com

A catalogue record for this book is available from the British
Library.

PB ISBN: 9781840025170
E ISBN: 9781786821980

Characters

TOBY
retired, said to be ninety-one, sprightly

RODERICK
his son, retired probably early, mid-fifties

ARIADNE
his daughter in law, Roderick's wife, late forties

DANIEL
his grandson, Roderick's son, ex-student, twenty-one

MOLLY
his cook/housekeeper, eighty-ish, heavily built

EMILY
his daily help, sixties, lightly built

JOYCE
Molly's great niece, ex-student, twenty-one

GERALD
his rich neighbour, early forties

The play is set in Toby's garden in northern Britain, on the nearby moors, and in Gerald's garden. It covers twenty-four hours.

Summer Again was first performed at the Orange Tree Theatre, on 6 October 2004, with the following cast:

TOBY, Robin Parkinson
RODERICK, Robert Benfield
ARIADNE, Miranda Foster
DANIEL, Jack Sandle
MOLLY, Eve Shickle
EMILY, Vilma Hollinbery
JOYCE, Octavia Walters
GERALD, David Leonard

Directed by Joyce Branagh
Designed by Sam Dowson

This version of the script was the one in use during the first two weeks of rehearsal, and could possibly have changed slightly during the remaining period.

ACT ONE

Scene 1

The scene is set in a garden with some chairs or seats. Revealed at the beginning are DANIEL, aged about 21, an ex-student, reading, and MOLLY, a cook, aged somewhere in the eighties, but looking younger. She is shelling peas.

The sound of a propeller driven aircraft causes both to look up. MOLLY looks to DANIEL and smiles. He neither notices nor responds.

Enter EMILY with a duster. She is younger than MOLLY and stringier. She shakes her duster.

EMILY: Don't mind me. I've done me brasses and me mantel pieces and now I'm shaking me duster. (*No reaction.*) I'm shaking me duster.

    MOLLY turns away. Offended, EMILY speaks to the audience.

    (*To the audience.*) I'm the daily help, bottom of the pile, and (*Referring to MOLLY.*) that's not healthy.

MOLLY: Who are you talking to?

EMILY: None of your business.

MOLLY: Then give over.

EMILY: (*To audience, as whispering.*) I go home at the end of the morning which it nearly is, and I expect that would suit them if it wasn't for his mother and father, and his grandmother and grandfather, the old fool who plans to buy the garden next door – over there – which will kill him because he's ninety-one. Well, it's not my business, because when I've finished, which I nearly have, I go home and they don't, so (*To the others.*) don't mind me, I'm shaking me duster.

She shakes her duster. No response from the others.

I've done me brasses and me mantel pieces, and now I'm shaking me duster.

No response. Goes on shaking the duster.

Don't mind me, will you. I've done me brasses and me mantel pieces and –

MOLLY: Whatever d'you mean, don't mind me?

EMILY: I'm just saying, don't let me get in your way.

MOLLY: You have done.

DANIEL: What are we doing you could get in the way of?

EMILY: You know very well what I mean, Molly.

DANIEL: *I* don't…

EMILY: You, ganging up, you and Mr Daniel.

DANIEL: I'm trying to read.

EMILY: Well, don't mind me, I'm going to do me hoovering. (*To audience.*) I told you, bottom of the pile, me.

MOLLY: Who d'you keep talking to?

EMILY: Nobody, and I've got me hoovering to do, and I'll do me shopping on the way home, if I've time.

MOLLY: It's only the dining room you're hoovering, not Buckingham Palace.

EMILY: There's no need to be rude.

MOLLY: I'm not being rude.

EMILY: She is, isn't she, Mr Daniel?

MOLLY: I'm not, am I Mr Daniel.

DANIEL: I'm trying to read.

EMILY: Well, she is, she's being rude, and I'm going to do me hoovering and then home.

MOLLY: To that Wilf, if only your mother will let him out of her sight for half a minute.

EMILY: I'm going to hoover.

MOLLY: What d'you get up to in the potting shed with that Wilf, then?

EMILY: We're very genteel.

MOLLY: If he can catch his breath. (*Imitation of bronchial breathing.*)

EMILY: Molly!

MOLLY: Not much cop kissing the lodger if he wheezes. When he puts his tongue down your throat I should think he sucks you half way down to his stomach.

EMILY: That's quite unnecessary.

MOLLY: At the other end, mind you, down there –

EMILY: Molly! We are not alone.

MOLLY: Mr Daniel? Tell us what you think of Wilf's breathing.

DANIEL: I've never heard it…

MOLLY: But you understood what I meant about the kissing and that.

DANIEL: Oh please.

EMILY: He's too well educated.

DANIEL: I have books to read.

EMILY: Well, don't mind me, I'll get out of your way. (*To audience.*) His grandfather's going to kill himself, you see.

She leaves. MOLLY watches her go.

DANIEL: What does she mean, she'll get out of our way? We aren't doing anything.

MOLLY: D'you like reading?

DANIEL: It's all right.

MOLLY: Why don't you go travelling? (*Nothing.*) You mustn't let your parents stand in your way, Mr Daniel.

DANIEL: I've told you, I have books to read.

MOLLY: Get your tail up and go off with that brassy faced crowd of yours.

DANIEL: They've gone already.

MOLLY: You could find someone. You've got lovely skin, Mr Daniel. Like a baby. (*She finishes shelling the peas.*) That's those little loves shelled, so now it's a nice lamb chop, peas and potatoes for lunch.

DANIEL: Again?

MOLLY: Eh?

DANIEL: Why do you always fight Emily?

MOLLY: What's wrong with lamb chop, peas and potatoes?

Enter RODERICK, aged about 45, DANIEL's father.

RODERICK: Ah, Daniel, Molly.

MOLLY: Sir.

DANIEL: Father.

RODERICK: Don't go.

MOLLY: There's lunch to do.

RODERICK: Lamb chop, peas and potatoes again. (*Light laugh.*)

MOLLY: You don't have to eat them. Excuse me.

She goes.

RODERICK: Did I say something?

DANIEL: You should know. She's part of your life, not mine. I've some things to do. (*Moves to go.*)

RODERICK: I was actually free once, Dan. I wasn't always a parent.

DANIEL: Got pissed over Vietnam and shagged like a rabbit outside American airbases. With commitment of course. Excuse me.

RODERICK: We were quite serious, really. (*Light laugh.*) Anyway, Molly's great niece is coming to visit, I believe. Nice girl, Joyce, young, pretty – young. What is it now?

DANIEL: Why do we visit here?

RODERICK: Because they love us. No, because we love them.

DANIEL: I don't.

RODERICK: I know, and it's a pity, really. You see, knowing another generation – there's great wisdom here, Dan. It's an inner thing they have.

DANIEL: I think I'd better go an make some notes.

RODERICK: You're avoiding me.

DANIEL: Yes.

RODERICK: I know you have your own life to lead –

DANIEL: So do you.

RODERICK: Yes, of course. What d'you mean?

DANIEL: You don't have to give your life to your parents.

RODERICK: It's very relaxing here in the hills, and that's why we come. And because I care about them.

DANIEL: I'll make my notes.

RODERICK: Daniel –

DANIEL: Don't bleat.

RODERICK: I don't bleat. What d'you mean, bleat?

DANIEL: You bleat.

RODERICK: Listen. In primitive tribes there were rites of passage where the older generation took the younger generation into a big hut and told them things. You know?

DANIEL: We aren't a primitive tribe. I know you'd like us to be so we could all take over where our ancestors left off, working away at the next small step for humanity, but all that's past. Dead. Finished. Over. It's not there now. There's no more wisdom, only power, naked power, and everything's bleak and I've got things to do. (*Moves.*)

RODERICK: I'm sure all that can't be entirely true, can it?

DANIEL: Of course it is. Nothing we think matters because we're run by other people who have guns and money. Aren't you worried by that?

RODERICK: Well –

DANIEL: Then think how I feel, with no wisdom, no guidance, only power blundering over everything, and grandfather droning on, and Molly and Emily being unintelligible.

RODERICK: Couldn't you feel liberated?

DANIEL: You mean enthusiastic?

RODERICK: There'd be some point to things if you were. I mean – what does it all mean? What does it all mean?

DANIEL: You keep saying that, and it's no way to bring up a son.

RODERICK: I know, but what does it all

DANIEL: Nothing. Can I go?

RODERICK: Of course.

DANIEL: Why don't you ever stop me?

RODERICK: If I stopped you, I'd have to talk to you. Look, perhaps at the moment we don't have a lot to say to each other, but –

DANIEL: Perhaps we have.

RODERICK: Oh? I thought you were going.

DANIEL: What wisdom is there in Emily? Why does she come here?

RODERICK: It's safe.

DANIEL: Who's this Wilf person? Who is her mother?

RODERICK: Dead.

DANIEL: They talk of her as if she's alive.

RODERICK: She's not.

DANIEL: Why are we up here, father?

RODERICK: Dad.

DANIEL: Why!

RODERICK: Oh, the longing to hear you say Dad.

DANIEL: Can't you get your head above sentimentality? Why are we here?

RODERICK: Why are *you* here, instead of getting a job?

DANIEL: I don't know.

RODERICK: Well you should.

DANIEL: I'm going.

RODERICK: There's the question of the garden, if you must know. I can't think why your grandfather wants an extra bit of garden at his age. He can hardly hold a hoe.

DANIEL: Does it matter?

RODERICK: Yes. It's half an acre of ornamental flower beds. The whole thing changes every week, and needs constant weeding, watering, whatever it is you have to do to gardens, mulching. And he won't employ a gardener, and he hates flowers. And Gerald Roberts doesn't want to sell it anyway, and there'll be a fuss. There's always a fuss.

DANIEL: I'll go to my notes.

RODERICK: Do you have to?

Enter MOLLY.

MOLLY: Lunch in fifteen minutes.

DANIEL: There's never any time.

MOLLY: I thought I'd tell you myself, because it's good and nourishing.

DANIEL: Thank you.

Enter EMILY in a hat.

EMILY: I've done me hoovering, and now I'm off.

MOLLY: I didn't hear you.

EMILY: I did it quietly so as not to disturb anyone.

RODERICK: You can't hoover quietly. You either do it and it's noisy, or you don't do it at all.

DANIEL: Oh, the agony.

RODERICK: Daniel –

MOLLY: What agony?

EMILY: I'm off before anyone calls me a liar to my face. Sir. Mr Daniel.

MOLLY: (*As she goes.*) And tell that Wilf to keep his tongue in his own mouth.

DANIEL: (*Also leaving.*) I don't know how you can bear it.

RODERICK: (*Calling.*) Because I'm used to it! (*To audience.*) Why doesn't he buzz off to Thailand or wherever it is they pretend to grow up these days? Or India, to gather insights? For me, it was Italy, the blessed flowering of proportion, not a warm mist of drugs and semen, endless letting go, moving on, getting drunk. What does it all mean? I know I mustn't keep saying that, but it is a question. What does it – I mean, what does it mean?

TOBY: (*Off.*) Nothing!

RODERICK: Oh God, I shouldn't have spoken.

Enter TOBY, 91, but looking spry.

TOBY: It's a piece of abstract art, very good to look at but difficult to experience if you're in the wrong bit of the canvas.

RODERICK: Yes I know, father. You've been saying so for years.

TOBY: And I've never met anyone who thought the same except a farmer near Harlech, which castle was built as a defence against the English.

RODERICK: Do shut up.

TOBY: If I shut up I'll die. The English were forever trying to colonise the Welsh, who turned Baptist to annoy them and even now speak in code to keep themselves separate from the occupying forces. If you want to stay alive you have to have a little plot of land where no-one else can understand you, and where you can develop an exquisitely narrow mind.

RODERICK: If you buy another bit of garden, your little plot will –

TOBY: I'll stay alive because I'll have to work. People say they'd never think I was ninety-one, and I've been sent out here to get you in for drinks before lunch, lamb chops, peas and potatoes because Molly doesn't know how to cook anything else. What she needs is a good man, though I can't think of one to recommend – you only had one son, and that was a surprise.

RODERICK: Who said so?

TOBY: I also ask myself what does it all mean, and the answer I get is nothing, but as always there are other things that are quite pretty – abstract art, Welsh shepherds and so on – so I might as well enjoy that garden while I can. Drinks.

RODERICK: How are you going to get it?

TOBY: Blackmail. Gerald Roberts, who owns it, has tampered with every willing woman in the town, and that doesn't look good on his CV for Chairmanship of the Round Table, so I'll teach him to go poking his nose in where he isn't wanted, except it wasn't his nose he went poking in, it was his –

RODERICK: Father!

TOBY: Sorry. I don't like being coarse. Oh dear.

RODERICK: It's all right.

TOBY: No, I'll pay him for it. A very decent sum.

Enter DANIEL.

DANIEL: Grandmother says it's nearly lunch.

TOBY: I know it's nearly lunch.

DANIEL: Why am I here?

RODERICK: We're coming in for drinks.

TOBY: I'm coming in for drinks.

16

DANIEL: Mother's pouring them.

TOBY: Who?

DANIEL: His wife.

TOBY: Whose wife?

DANIEL: Father's.

RODERICK: Your daughter in law.

TOBY: I know who she is.

DANIEL: And then it's lamb chops.

TOBY: Lamb chops.

RODERICK: Lamb chops.

TOBY: Welsh, probably, grown near Harlech. And I can chomp at them because I've got my own teeth. I shall spread a rumour that Gerald Roberts is raising greenfly in large quantities. That'll scupper him at the golf club.

He is off.

DANIEL: Wisdom? Love?

A propeller driven aircraft again causes the men to look up.

RODERICK: Propeller driven. It takes me back.

DANIEL: Back where, for God's sake?

He leaves.

RODERICK: Well, there's not much point in going forward, apparently.

He leaves.

Scene 2

A lighting change. Enter ARIADNE, RODERICK's wife, and JOYCE, aged the same as DANIEL. JOYCE holds two cups of coffee.

ARIADNE: It's a cocoon here, really. You know what a cocoon is?

JOYCE: Yes.

ARIADNE: Don't mess it about or things die in it. And that was lunch, so there are only six more before we can go home. I'm Daniel's mother.

JOYCE: D'you know who I am?

ARIADNE: You're Joyce, Molly's great niece. Aren't you?

JOYCE: Yes, I am.

ARIADNE: You've grown, but you still ate in the kitchen.

JOYCE: Yes, I did.

ARIADNE: I hope you had enough.

JOYCE: Yes, thank you.

ARIADNE: Don't you find the M1 is always so crowded?

JOYCE: I don't have a car.

ARIADNE: I don't know why we go that way, I've said, it's better if we go late at night or early in the morning, but we're trapped by grandfather always knowing better, and you can't get a word in edgeways. I don't know why we put up with it, except the bluebells are wonderful, and the moors, and the brown water's so clear, coming off the peat. I hate it being cold, but it is refreshing and lovely in autumn, and the M1 is quick if there isn't an oil leak, which there was once, but that was a different car and besides the firm went broke.

JOYCE: Coffee?

ARIADNE: I'm one of those women whose possibilities were terminally restricted by marriage. You know about the war, of course.

JOYCE: Which one?

ARIADNE: The one that made our Prime Minister mad.

JOYCE: He says it's been a victory.

ARIADNE: Ah! Hahaha!

JOYCE: Did it make you mad, too?

ARIADNE: No, I'm always like this. I do amateur drama, and we're all wonderfully mad in amateur drama. 'I'm a tree.' No, the war made me sane. It was the Prime Minister who went mad.

JOYCE: You think he did the wrong thing?

ARIADNE: Of course. Mad for heroism, passionate to be thought sincere, hopelessly believing everything he says – odd from a public school boy.

JOYCE: It seems typical to me.

ARIADNE: (*Taking a cup.*) Thank you.

JOYCE: Of course, Daniel went to Lancing.

ARIADNE: Are you married yet? Or do you flit from relationship to relationship like a young bee?

JOYCE: I came to see Daniel.

ARIADNE: He didn't eat in the kitchen.

JOYCE: No.

ARIADNE: And you didn't eat in the dining room.

JOYCE: Molly said not to.

ARIADNE: Aunt Molly.

JOYCE: Actually Molly.

ARIADNE: Really?

JOYCE: Where do you live?

ARIADNE: In the south. That's why the M1 –

JOYCE: Yes, I know. Chelsea. I meant in what sort of world?

ARIADNE: Chelsea. Don't tamper with it. We all need our warrens to pop in and out of.

JOYCE: Don't you feel lost in the open?

ARIADNE: Don't, just don't, that's all. We get vicious if tampered with. And I'm really hoping for a lover.

JOYCE: Why?

ARIADNE: The usual reason, I imagine.

JOYCE: You just want someone to come inside you?

ARIADNE: No! Well, someone else. People do it, you know. Especially in amateur drama. Look, I do have values – I know you shouldn't have eaten in the kitchen, though where else, I mean she is related to you and – and anyway, I want a lover because – because – the thrill. Quick, let it be Tuesday, that sort of thing. You don't know about that?

JOYCE: I only sleep with people I love.

ARIADNE: Doesn't that lead to lying?

JOYCE: Not yet.

ARIADNE: Oh. Well, the only good thing about this new garden grandfather wants is that lovely Gerald Roberts will probably call round and – you shouldn't know this.

JOYCE: Then don't tell me.

ARIADNE: I have to, otherwise – . Gerald is the owner of the garden and grandfather's neighbour, and he – he –

JOYCE: Sleeps around?

ARIADNE: I hope so. And if he comes, and this is the point, I hope you, and everyone else, will keep out of the way, despite the fact he approved of the war, which will only add a certain *je ne sais quoi* – oh Molly.

MOLLY has entered with a cup of coffee.

MOLLY: I'm sorry about the state of the dining room, madam, but Emily said she was hoovering it.

ARIADNE: I didn't notice.

MOLLY: I expect she forgot again. Oh, you've got coffee.

ARIADNE: If Mr Roberts calls and Mr and Mrs Toby are asleep, I'm out here.

MOLLY: Perhaps if you tell Mr and Mrs Toby that I think Emily is idle –

ARIADNE: That's not my business.

MOLLY: In that case I'll try and find someone who wants this. (*To JOYCE.*) And you look out for yourself. I'm making a picnic. (*Nods meaningfully and leaves.*)

ARIADNE: What does that mean?

JOYCE: You all seem preoccupied with different things from me, but I'm trying to be civilised, so don't force me to talk.

ARIADNE: What a busy little speech. Is this because of my wanting a lover?

JOYCE: It's because –

ARIADNE: You can't take the idea of middle-aged lust, snogging amid the double chins?

JOYCE: No, it's because –

ARIADNE: Are you by any chance a lesbian?

JOYCE: No.

ARIADNE: That might've tidied things up.

JOYCE: It's because you're Daniel's quite young mother and have elderly attitudes.

ARIADNE: I was against the war.

JOYCE: Everyone was.

ARIADNE: You're tampering, I knew you would. Are you friends with Daniel?

JOYCE: We meet from time to time.

ARIADNE: Well, it's a lovely idea, to meet, of course. How do you come to do it?

JOYCE: We both went to Lancaster.

ARIADNE: What for? Oh, the university. Daniel did go there – was it nice?

JOYCE: Well –

ARIADNE: I wish he'd get a job.

JOYCE: He's writing a book, and that takes everything he has.

ARIADNE: Is that much?

JOYCE: Don't you know?

ARIADNE: Not really.

JOYCE: Well, let me say that there's more to Daniel than there sometimes seems.

ARIADNE: I'm so glad.

MOLLY: (*Re-entering, still with coffee.*) Mr Roberts is here, so perhaps you'll mention Emily –

TOBY enters with GERALD ROBERTS, 45 or so, self-satisfied, with a lap top which he opens.

TOBY: Mrs Toby's asleep, which is good because she can't interfere, and this is Ariadne, as you know, and this is Joyce – where are Daniel and Roderick?

MOLLY: They're avoiding each other.

TOBY: (*Sitting.*) Well, I can't afford much but here's my offer and I want it kept secret.

He hands over a piece of paper.

MOLLY: You could offer more if you cut down on staff.

TOBY: Are you going to retire?

MOLLY: Me?

TOBY: What's that computer doing here? There's no electricity.

GERALD: It runs on a battery.

TOBY: Like a flashlight?

JOYCE: I'd better go and find Daniel.

MOLLY: It was Emily I was talking about.

TOBY: When?

MOLLY: Just now.

TOBY: I didn't hear.

MOLLY: Then I'll get the picnic.

TOBY: What picnic?

MOLLY: They're going up to the moors.

JOYCE: Who says?

TOBY: It's a lovely day for it, so thank you, Molly.

GERALD: We'll meet again, of course.

JOYCE: Are you Gerald?

ARIADNE: Yes, he is.

GERALD: Yes. Good afternoon, Ariadne. Have you recovered from winning the war?

JOYCE: It isn't won, exactly.

MOLLY: Picnic.

JOYCE: Yes, but –

MOLLY: (*To ARIADNE.*) And don't forget about Emily.

JOYCE and MOLLY exit, MOLLY leading her by the arm.

JOYCE: Leave Emily alone.

TOBY: What did she say?

ARIADNE: Leave Emily alone.

TOBY: Why?

ARIADNE: She's that sort of girl. How nice to see you, again, Gerald. And bygones should be bygones.

GERALD: (*At his lap top.*) E-mails, e-mails. Clutter all the time.

TOBY: Do kiss if you want to. I shall fall asleep, probably.

ARIADNE: Grandfather –

TOBY: I'm not your grandfather, and he does it with everyone. It's the thing in the golf club set. I'll just sit here and watch, or fall asleep.

ARIADNE: I can't.

TOBY: Don't be so negative.

ARIADNE: I feel embarrassed.

TOBY: I've seen everything in my time, especially after the war, in Hamburg. Go on, you're a liberal…

GERALD: (*At his computer.*) So, Ariadne. We liberated a dictatorship.

ARIADNE: What? Oh, yes. So we did. And your hair shook so patriotically on the platform for those in favour of whatever it was – bombs I think. I'm not being ironical, Gerald. Your hair is very convincing. There are times – Are you asleep yet?

TOBY: No.

ARIADNE: Nearly, or not nearly?

TOBY: Quite nearly.

ARIADNE: Well, shut your eyes.

TOBY: Just get on with it.

GERALD: Get on with what? Rejecting his offer?

ARIADNE: No, no, let's consider it for a moment.

GERALD: I have done.

ARIADNE: But there are other things to think about before – before Roddy turns up.

GERALD: What things?

ARIADNE: Grandfather? Father in law? (*TOBY is asleep.*) Ah. Well now, shall I be frank, Gerald? I – I love you. There. I love you.

GERALD: (*At his computer still.*) I'm not really into love.

ARIADNE: No. Well, actually I'm not suggesting love, not as such, though of course you are lovable.

GERALD: (*At his computer still.*) It's pretty ghastly to be loved.

ARIADNE: Is it? I can't remember. Do stop fiddling – Oh. I'm sorry.

GERALD: Actually you don't seem to have the tiny threads necessary for communicating love.

ARIADNE: Oh, I have, I have. I'm full of threads, like a spider. Oh no, that's the wrong comparison.

TOBY: Yes.

ARIADNE: Grandfather?

TOBY: I'm nearly off.

GERALD: Being loved is very like being held in a spider's web, I've always found.

ARIADNE: I've always thought it was like curling up in front of the fire. Muffins for tea kind of thing. Perhaps you don't remember what it's like being in front of the fire, since you're probably all electric. Toby?

GERALD: I have a fire-place.

ARIADNE: Oh good. Either shut that up, or leave it alone.

GERALD: I have a business to run.

ARIADNE: I'm sorry. I'm actually probably just trying to be friends. Friends with sex thrown in.

GERALD: You don't know where you are, do you.

ARIADNE: Yes, I do. I hate the American President.

GERALD: Because he does know where he is?

ARIADNE: Does he?

GERALD: (*Turning from his computer.*) Let's be frank. What you are is desirable. Not overwhelmingly but more than average.

ARIADNE: Oh! And are you going to desire me, Gerald? Please?

TOBY's eyes open for a second.

GERALD: Like the American President, I do know what I want. And what you want. And what you shall have. But it won't be love.

ARIADNE: What will it be?

GERALD: Very high quality. Sweet Ariadne.

He kisses her. She squeaks a little with delight in mid-kiss. TOBY smiles 'Ah' and goes back to sleep.

ARIADNE: (*Still kissing.*) More.

Still kissing, GERALD laughs lightly.

GERALD: I knew you'd like it.

Enter RODERICK.

RODERICK: I thought you were against the war, Ariadne.

Kiss breaks.

ARIADNE: Oh Roddy. We're making our peace.

GERALD: Do you mind, Roderick?

RODERICK: Well – what – I mean what does it all –

ARIADNE: You're not to say that, it drives me mad. Why don't you go for a walk on the moors?

TOBY: (*In his sleep.*) Off you go, all of you.

ARIADNE: Grandfather?

TOBY: I'm asleep.

RODERICK: (*Of the computer.*) Shall I turn that off? Save the battery?

GERALD: I'll do it.

RODERICK: Oh. Right. Look, we don't want him to buy the garden, Gerald.

GERALD: The price is a good deal more than he's offered so –

RODERICK: Oh right! Well. The moors then.

ARIADNE: I love you, Roddy.

RODERICK: Oh good. Me too. You, that is – I love you. Bye.

He goes.

GERALD: That was permission, wasn't it.

ARIADNE: I expect the dining room's free.

GERALD: I'm not interested in love, but I'm not interested either in an up against the wall job. There's only high quality practice for me, dear, and that requires time and complete privacy, not a headlong rush to the groin.

ARIADNE: Friendship with a dash of –

GERALD: No. I'm talking about high quality practice.

ARIADNE: Don't you have friends?

GERALD: Friends?

ARIADNE: There are things called friends, Gerald. I have amateur dramatic friends. They don't approve of the war, either, and we have coffee together and go on marches and sometimes quite like young people.

GERALD: Are you coming out for the afternoon with me, in my car, to the moors, or aren't you? As I say, you are desirable, and I'd like to find out what that's all about.

ARIADNE: As a friend.

GERALD: Your skin is lovely.

ARIADNE: Like Daniel's.

GERALD: Come along, Ariadne.

ARIADNE: Oh. Well, I suppose this is it.

They leave.

TOBY: (*Eyes shut.*) If you don't sell your bit of garden, I may very well die and it'll be your fault. Hello? I thought there was someone listening to me.

Enter MOLLY with the cup of coffee.

MOLLY: I've brought you this, Mr Toby. (*Gives coffee.*)

TOBY: Have I been repeating myself?

MOLLY: It's about the staff. We have too many, and some don't do any work to speak of and what we have to do is get rid of them. Good money after bad, is Emily.

TOBY: She's not a lot of money.

MOLLY: She doesn't need it, Mr Toby, with Wilf drawing his pension and his sickness pay, and her mother being –

TOBY: Dead.

MOLLY: So let Emily have her peace now. It'll be the best thing.

TOBY: (*Of the coffee.*) This is cold, and I like Emily.

MOLLY: She's not up to it any more, what with Wilf and all that.

TOBY: Why didn't you get married?

MOLLY: That's private.

TOBY: You were too bossy, I suppose. I don't mind, because you hold us all together like the ivy on the front, dusty, but if you pulled it down the mortar would fall out. We abandoned ourselves to you years ago.

MOLLY: Is that how it is.

TOBY: Well, the words just came out. I wonder if Gerald Roberts has sold me his garden?

MOLLY: You don't want his garden.

TOBY: Yes, I do.

MOLLY: No.

TOBY: Were you ever in love?

MOLLY: He was a minor canon of Derby cathedral, name of Ducane. And he loved me. Years before I came to you and Mrs Toby.

TOBY: You were always a ruin in our house. Well, tea time next.

MOLLY: And you've drunk your coffee. I'll get you some scones.

TOBY: Oh God, you've made scones, how dreadful.

MOLLY: Everyone else is on the moors, so you and Mrs Toby can have a real feast.

TOBY: (*As they go.*) What are you up to with Daniel?

MOLLY: He's a lovely lad…

TOBY: Well, don't soil him.

MOLLY: There's a nasty word, Mr Toby.

TOBY: You're a nasty woman and you make awful scones.

They are off.

Scene 3

Enter to the moors DANIEL and JOYCE with picnic basket.

DANIEL: If you've come up here simply to complain about eating in the kitchen –

JOYCE: You're hopelessly woven into what your ridiculous mother likes to call a cocoon, and I see no hope of you ever leaving it as a butterfly. Possibly a silk worm, dead in the water, but that's as far –

DANIEL: Oh, do shut up.

JOYCE: You didn't even ask if I wanted to eat in the kitchen.

DANIEL: Well, Molly is your great aunt, and family is family.

JOYCE: And lovers are lovers.

DANIEL: But there are protocols.

JOYCE: For lovers?

DANIEL: It's just the kitchen is where you belong – no,

come from – no, it's just she is your great aunt. Oh God. Look, I know they're addled, set in aspic, hopeless. I know. I know! I quarrelled with my father about it this morning – Molly, Emily, grandparents –

JOYCE: And you haven't told them about us.

DANIEL: I expect they realise.

JOYCE: Your mother didn't even know we'd met.

DANIEL: I expect she did, really. She's in amateur dramatics. Now listen. At this moment, there's a part of me that's almost exuberant, which is rare, and I want to share it with you. There is nothing, absolutely nothing, that is so emancipating as peeing in the open, which I have just done, with considerable panache, and it makes me feel part of nature – trees, animals, birds, everything like that.

JOYCE: Are you being romantic?

DANIEL: Oh God no. Romantics are losers, always wailing – don't leave me, I Believe in Yesterday, Mull of Kintyre, Puccini – they're all throbbing with grief. Every time that student starts to sing Your Tiny Hand Is Frozen I want to stand up in the stalls and shout, 'Leave him alone love, go and do something practical, like standing by the radiator.'

JOYCE: Do you often sit in the stalls?

DANIEL: Are you going to tell me to get a job?

JOYCE: How's the book?

DANIEL: You are going to tell me to get a job. I'm on chapter two.

JOYCE: I want to talk.

DANIEL: Well, it's interesting about grief, because people love it more than they do happiness.

JOYCE: That's not what I want to talk about.

DANIEL: When Princess Diana died everyone was really pleased. The nation's favourite waif swept up to the stars with her boy friend – 'Princess Killed In Mercedes Crash In Paris' – yummy. No-one would have been half so happy with headlines saying 'Princess fabulous in frantic sex frolic', which was the actual situation at the time. The fact is, we're born sad, but every once in a while, like just now, peeing in the heather –

JOYCE: (*Of supermarket packages she is taking out of the picnic basket.*) Where did she get all this?

DANIEL: I was talking. I was telling truths about certain bits of life.

JOYCE: It's all from Tesco's, and she says she never goes to supermarkets. It's poor Emily who goes to supermarkets.

DANIEL: Does this matter?

JOYCE: It's been in the freezer. She's been planning it.

DANIEL: Oh.

JOYCE: (*She takes out a piece of paper.*) 'Let me not to the marriage of true minds admit impediment.'

DANIEL: Molly wrote that?

JOYCE: In copper plate.

DANIEL: Molly?

JOYCE: She did go to school.

DANIEL: Yes but poetry –

JOYCE: No-one dared talk about love at Lancing, I suppose, full of the nation's richer waifs, gazing at the prefects like young does.

DANIEL: Oh, we really are talking about class, now, are

we. The world is coming to an end and you worry
about –

JOYCE: If I walk off these moors and into a bus never to
see you again, will it ever occur to you to think about
your tone of voice?

DANIEL: If you're suggesting I should be so
condescending as to drop my middle-class accent –

JOYCE: Tell me what you think this picnic means.

DANIEL: No.

JOYCE: Why not?

DANIEL: I suppose it could mean that your great aunt
wants you and me to get off together. It could be a kind
of wedding feast.

JOYCE: Think of the effort that went in to getting it,
hiding it in the freezer, paying for it. Has she never said
anything?

DANIEL: I only see her on these ghastly visits. She did
say today that I had lovely skin. (*Laughs.*) People do. I
suppose she and I know how things work, who counts,
who doesn't.

JOYCE: Who does?

DANIEL: Let's leave it.

JOYCE: No.

DANIEL: Why not?

JOYCE: Because I want to understand.

DANIEL: It's food, that's all, disgusting supermarket pre-
cooked food. Stomachfuls of stuff that kills you with E
numbers and calories and all those unimaginative things
my book's about.

JOYCE: Is it?

DANIEL: It might be.

JOYCE: If you write it. Why did she do this?

DANIEL: I've no idea and I can't be bothered to find out. There. Can't be bothered. That's me, isn't it. Well, it's hard to be bothered with the world coming to an end.

JOYCE: Perhaps she loves you.

DANIEL: Me? Loved by a really ancient cook?

JOYCE: What's so wrong with cooks?

DANIEL: What did you talk about in the kitchen, about me? What did she say about me?

JOYCE: That you have lovely skin.

DANIEL: Well, I've told you, people do say that.

JOYCE: Do you tell people what lovely things I have?

DANIEL: Only close friends. Those things are intimate, you know.

JOYCE: Perhaps this picnic is my great aunt being intimate with you.

DANIEL: Oh God. Frankfurters.

JOYCE: Hasn't anyone noticed how she feels towards you?

DANIEL: I think Emily – I think she thinks we're involved somehow, but we're not.

JOYCE: Your mother?

DANIEL: She's not into – I mean it's all disgusting.

JOYCE: Your mother is looking for a lover in Gerald Roberts.

DANIEL: She's not.

JOYCE: Daniel! Can't you open your eyes to anything that's going on around you? This place is seething like a snake pit and you don't pick up any of it.

DANIEL: I do! I told my father this morning, it's all pointless, the world is going to end.

JOYCE: And what are you doing about it?

DANIEL: Writing a book.

JOYCE: Chapter two.

DANIEL: Well, you have to go through chapter two to reach chapter three.

JOYCE: I used to think you could actually be useful, but really, I begin to wonder.

DANIEL: (*He has picked up some food and is nibbling at it.*) Are you going to rescue me?

JOYCE: I don't think I can.

DANIEL: That's another sad thing people do. They find wounded other people and decide to save them. I'm wounded, of course, the better off always are.

JOYCE: Talk to me positively about peeing in the heather.

DANIEL: Not now. I wish I hadn't eaten that. It feels as if I've consummated something I'd rather not have. Are you really leaving?

JOYCE: I've put a lot into this relationship.

DANIEL: So have I, but the world really *is* going to end, melting away under our duvets, disappearing as we laugh and make love and shop at Sainsbury's.

JOYCE: And what about our children?

DANIEL: Our what?

JOYCE: Under the duvet one lively little sperm might just get lost and meet an errant egg and biology might get to work without either of us noticing.

DANIEL: Are you telling me something?

JOYCE: If we have to face the fact that we have brought another generation into a dying world, what are you going to do?

DANIEL: Has it happened?

JOYCE: Suppose it has?

DANIEL: I'm not supposing, I'm asking.

JOYCE: I'm not telling.

DANIEL: Why not?

JOYCE: I want to know what you'd say if it had.

DANIEL: I'd be nonplussed.

JOYCE: Anything else?

DANIEL: I haven't got a job yet. And I haven't got beyond chapter two. And I'm still learning – I read all the time, I could be a teacher if I tried.

JOYCE: I am a teacher.

DANIEL: Trainee. Infant. I'm talking the real stuff.

JOYCE: So am I.

DANIEL: The world is going to end, Joyce. Don't you realise? Doesn't anyone realise?

JOYCE: So what are you going to do if I'm pregnant?

DANIEL: Well, there's not much point in your having it if the world's going –

JOYCE: That's my decision, or would be if I really –

DANIEL: I couldn't ever make love to you again if I thought you might get careless about having –

JOYCE: Women have had babies for centuries in the near certainty that they would die in childbirth or the babies would die in their wombs, or of plague, or be born crooked, or –

DANIEL: They lived in primitive times.

JOYCE: They inspired great love poems in the men who killed them. All those orgasms leading to the grave – not very different from the situation you're suggesting. Even Molly seems to know something about it.

DANIEL: She's not pregnant. I mean she couldn't be.

JOYCE: What are you going to do about her?

DANIEL: Nothing! Are you or are you not pregnant?

JOYCE: I have no intention of telling you until you tell me what you would do if you had to face something that wasn't just hatched up in your head?

DANIEL: The end of the world is not just hatched up in my head, it's happening.

JOYCE: So what would you do about facing extinction if you had a child?

DANIEL: The logical thing would be to strangle it. Yes, well, I can see that you wouldn't want to do that.

JOYCE: No.

DANIEL: But the world is already melting, and the gases, the ozone layer, the destruction of vegetation –

JOYCE: I know. You've told me, hundreds of times.

DANIEL: Then why –

JOYCE: Wouldn't you at least join something? Or build a raft? Or find a cave?

DANIEL: You sound exactly like my father.

JOYCE: Your father will be dead before the world ends. So I hope will your mother, even though she marched against the war.

DANIEL: She's a very clever amateur actress.

JOYCE: I don't know why I look to you for things. It's something to do with bodies. They signal to other bodies and minds don't have much to do with it. That leads to the sad music you hate, because eventually minds wake up, and they interfere, and the sweet sex stuff goes sour and won't work any more.

DANIEL: Are we separating?

JOYCE: D'you want to?

DANIEL: Just when I've had my epiphany moment in the heather. Of course I don't want to, but that hasn't anything to do with it.

Enter RODERICK.

RODERICK: Ah. Hello. No, don't move, I'm just passing. Aren't you going to say 'Do stay'?

DANIEL: No.

RODERICK: Right. You look a bit defeated, Dan. Anything I can do?

DANIEL: No.

RODERICK: Right. The course of true love never did –

DANIEL: Yes, I know.

RODERICK: Right. You know everything, of course. Must be quite alarming. (*Laughs. No-one else does.*) Sorry. Right. That's the family picnic basket, by the way. I remember it from – sorry. See you later.

He leaves, taking some food.

DANIEL: You see? He doesn't take me seriously.

JOYCE: (*Nothing.*)

DANIEL: We should all take each other seriously,

JOYCE: Including this. (*The picnic.*)

DANIEL: That makes me feel ill.

JOYCE: I've said everything about us, I think. We can go back to your house or we can talk about something different – the war, for instance.

DANIEL: We know about the war and it was all wrong and the American President blah blah blah – I'm bored with it.

JOYCE: (*Furious.*) The war was entirely about not taking people seriously. It was simply childish revenge taken by a man hidden from other people by his devotion to wealth. It lacked any kind of serious care for humanity, any attempt to understand the weaknesses that break people apart, any long stubborn view of where the messes come from in human enterprises – (*Slapping his face.*) – Daniel, don't you understand?

DANIEL: Yes, I've said so.

JOYCE: But have you felt so?

DANIEL: My cheek hurts, Joyce.

JOYCE: The end of the world – can't you be original?

DANIEL: The end of the world is very original. It'll only happen once.

Enter GERALD and ARIADNE, he with his laptop.

ARIADNE: I'm exhausted, and uncomfortable.

JOYCE: You didn't like it, then.

ARIADNE: We're rather tired, that's all.

GERALD: I said we'd meet again.

ARIADNE: Gerald, you're omnivorous

DANIEL: I think we've got some things left to say to each other.

JOYCE: Like goodbye.

GERALD: I hope not.

DANIEL: We've had a row, and I think we need to say things that will make us feel better, so excuse us. There's a picnic there, if you want it.

DANIEL leads JOYCE off.

ARIADNE: A row? I suspected they were lovers – No, Gerald, I've got heather sticking into all sorts of things.

GERALD: You cried out in ecstacy.

ARIADNE: I told you, the heather. Of course, the experience was interesting.

GERALD: There's usually a more rapturous response than that.

ARIADNE: I wonder if I'm designed for rapture. Why are you taking your shirt off again?

GERALD: It's incredibly hot.

DANIEL re-enters.

DANIEL: Excuse me, I'll take some sausage rolls.

ARIADNE: Stay here, Daniel. And don't take anything else off.

GERALD: It's so nice being naked on the moors. (*Begins to loosen zip.*)

ARIADNE: But familiarity breeds contempt. Do that up. (*She wrestles with him to get the zip done up.*)

DANIEL: Excuse me, Joyce is rather hungry.

He exits.

ARIADNE: Now look what you've done. He'll go and blether to the cook's great niece, for heaven's sake. No, don't take anything else – (*Renewed struggle over zip.*)

We've had enough. Gerald! (*It is done up.*) Sometimes
I understand very clearly the reasons for not invading
Iraq.

GERALD: Look, you come up North regularly to see the
old man, I come down South regularly on business –

ARIADNE: That sounds too much like marriage. (*Throws
a chicken leg to him.*) Eat that and then play with your
computer.

GERALD: I don't play, I run a modern business. I'm a
leader as I think you might have realized by now.

ARIADNE: You were like an ancient steam engine, The
Flying Scotsman. Is that what you call high quality?

GERALD: Yes. And you were good, which was a surprise.

ARIADNE: I'd like to talk about something else.

GERALD: The war was right, weapons of mass destruction
or no weapons of mass destruction, and the Iraqis are
probably grateful so God Bless America, and how
marvelous that you go at sex like –

ARIADNE: No, something else.

Enter DANIEL.

What now?

DANIEL: (*Taking a thermos flask.*) Joyce wants some tea.

ARIADNE: Was she shocked about –

DANIEL: Apparently you talked to her.

GERALD: And now we're talking about the war because
there's nothing else we have in common…

ARIADNE: I want to talk about the garden.

DANIEL: (*Leaving.*) I can't believe it.

GERALD: He's probably not going to have it.

ARIADNE: Good.

GERALD: His offer was ridiculous…

ARIADNE: It would kill him if he had it.

GERALD: And you don't want that?

ARIADNE: He and old grandma belong together to the end. What would she do without him?

GERALD: She'd live with you, Ariadne. She hates Molly. (*Continues at his computer.*)

Appalled silence from ARIADNE.

ARIADNE: It would be very cruel if he had your garden, Gerald. Everyone would hate it if he killed himself trying to do something he no longer could. Put that (*The computer.*) away – you're always somewhere else. Listen. It would be depressing for us all if Toby died trying to keep that garden beautiful, the way you do, because he can't. We should all stick to what we can do – don't misunderstand me – and although he's a dreadfully dominating old thing, with his road directions and his endless advice, he is at least alive, mostly. And living in a happy nest with his beloved wife. One shouldn't tamper with life and death.

GERALD: So what would you do to stop me selling to him?

Enter JOYCE, remaining unseen.

ARIADNE: No, Gerald, no more high quality.

GERALD: I've nothing to lose. I could easily put it about in the golf club how I found out you're a real goer. And when I come south next I could breathe a word or two in ears that belong to your circle –

ARIADNE: You wouldn't.

GERALD: On the other hand I could put it about that

42

you're not a real goer but more of a wet blanket. Which would you prefer?

ARIADNE: Do you have to keep working at that keyboard?

GERALD: I'm buying supermarkets in South East Asia.

ARIADNE: Why don't you have an egg and cress sandwich and – No, Gerald. No. Oh – oh – if you must.

GERALD kisses her. Both enjoy it, with squeaks. Enter RODERICK.

RODERICK: Oh bloody hell.

ARIADNE: For heaven's sake, Roddy, what are you thinking of?

RODERICK: Wherever I go looking for peace there's always someone else there and you're kissing them. I only came back for a nibble. (*He takes something from the picnic.*)

JOYCE: We've got some tea if you want.

RODERICK: Oh thank you. And hello again.

GERALD: (*To JOYCE.*) Don't go.

RODERICK: We are married, Ariadne, or had you forgotten?

ARIADNE: I'm having private discussions with Gerald, and do your shirt up.

RODERICK: It's hot.

ARIADNE: And you've a crumb on your –

RODERICK: Do you still love me?

ARIADNE: Of course I do. Oh Roderick, how could you think I don't?

RODRERICK: Because you keep kissing Gerald.

ARIADNE: That was a mistake, but what's done is done. And finished, isn't it Gerald.

RODERICK: Is it? (*GERALD is at his computer.*) It isn't, is it, Gerald.

ARIADNE: Gerald? Leave that computer. It's all over, isn't it.

Enter DANIEL.

DANIEL: What's happening now?

GERALD: Things always depend on other things. For instance, how anxious are you for your father not to buy my bit of garden?

RODERICK: Very.

GERALD: Yes. Well, I was very surprised, you see, by how sturdy Ariadne could be considering she's a liberal. You're a very lucky man.

RODERICK: I know. What do you mean?

ARIADNE: We're simply friends, Roddy. Just friends, aren't we Gerald.

GERALD: I don't have friends. I'm bowled over by Ariadne's originality, Roddy, really, amazing.

RODERICK: What did she – no, don't tell me.

ARIADNE: He's misunderstood things, deliberately. He simply wants to – it's to do with whether he accepts your father's offer for the garden.

RODERICK: How?

GERALD: I won't be far away if you need me.

He takes his computer to another part of the stage.

DANIEL: Mother I can't believe this.

JOYCE: I can. No wonder you're so odd.

ARIADNE: He's very clever and loving.

JOYCE: Just separate and be grown up. (*Exits.*)

DANIEL: Separate, move on, achieve normality. (*Exits.*)

RODERICK and ARIADNE speak almost in whispers.

RODERICK: What are they talking about?

ARIADNE: Suffering, and how to ignore it.

RODERICK: I knew there'd be a fuss.

ARIADNE: I want to go away.

RODERICK: Where to?

ARIADNE: A place where I can start again.

RODERICK: I've only just retired, and started on Proust.

ARIADNE: I have this awful fear the world might be in a mess, and I should do more about it than belong to the Dolphin Square Amateur Players.

RODERICK: You did march against the war.

ARIADNE: My intentions are often good.

RODERICK: Is this because of – of –

ARIADNE: He says I'm good at it, but I don't like it. Oh Roddy.

RODERICK: There. Finish your sandwich.

ARIADNE: No thank you. (*RODERICK takes it.*) And now he's going to sell Toby the garden if I don't do it again, and your father will die of over exertion and your mother will come to live with us – I'll have to sacrifice myself one way or another. Better to Gerald do you think?

RODERICK: You could always shut your eyes and pretend it was one of those improvisations you do at the Players.

ARIADNE: I want to be someone like Nurse Cavell or Rosa Luxemburg, the one that has a statue outside the National Portrait Gallery because she was brave and got shot for it.

RODERICK: Shall we creep away?

ARIADNE: What d'you think Molly's up to with Emily?

RODERICK: What d'you think she's up to with Daniel?

ARIADNE: D'you know Molly's great niece and Daniel both went to Lancaster?

RODERICK: What for? Oh yes. It's the modern world, Ariadne. Everybody's equal now.

ARIADNE: I wonder if that's the problem?

RODERICK: They say it's the solution.

ARIADNE: There are some funny people moving into Chelsea. Very clever. And of course young.

They go.

GERALD: (*Calling while at the lap-top.*) I heard you, and you'll be back! You like things to stay the way they are, so you'll let me in, cowards.

DANIEL has returned.

You'll be back.

DANIEL: I am back.

GERALD: Where's your girl friend?

DANIEL: (*Taking a biscuit.*) She thinks you're a joke.

GERALD: Oh dear.

DANIEL: She thinks I am too. What are you doing?

GERALD: I'm buying supermarkets in South East Asia.

DANIEL: Why?

GERALD: To make money.

DANIEL: Do people use supermarkets in South East Asia?

GERALD: Only small ones. I'm going to buy them up and turn them into big ones. Why does Joyce think I'm a joke?

DANIEL: Why are you turning small super markets into big ones?

GERALD: So that I can sell the people of South East Asia large fridges to store their food because they've changed their shopping habits. Once a week shopping will save hours of walking through the jungle, and make me more money than I could possibly spend.

DANIEL: And contribute to global warming.

GERALD: Yes.

DANIEL: You don't care?

GERALD: No.

DANIEL: Why not?

GERALD: Because I can have what opinions I want because I live in a free country. Also if the world *is* going to end, I want to have a lot of fun before it does, so shut up.

DANIEL: That's why you do what you do with my mother.

GERALD: (*Still at his lap-top.*) Yes.

DANIEL: Oh.

GERALD: And anyway there's going to be a meteorite which is going to kill us all quite soon, so there's nothing we can do, is there.

DANIEL: If you don't put your shirt on you'll get cancer of the skin.

GERALD: I'll get hot and sweaty if I put my shirt on,

DANIEL: Joyce likes people who are sweaty. (*Suddenly throwing away what he is eating.*) Oh can't you see? Green house gases, lack of oxygen from trees, sudden melting of the ice floes, tidal waves as snow falls off the mountains, land slips, destabilisation of the soil, the pall of carbon emissions, it's all happening now, this second, we're doomed, doomed.

GERALD: Might as well have sex, then.

DANIEL: With my mother. I'm actually writing a book. It won't get finished, of course.

GERALD: At least I'm improving the lives of the South East Asians, even if it means spoiling their poverty, so loved by tourists.

DANIEL: There'll still be millions of them on rubbish dumps, selling their sisters and their brothers.

GERALD: To me, probably. (*Turning from lap top.*) Look, I'm a shit, I expect my mother bottle fed me. (*Starting to pull on shirt.*) And now I'm ready to become hot and sweaty for Joyce, so –

DANIEL: I wouldn't bother. You have everything, and she doesn't like that sort of thing.

GERALD: I bet she does. The young are very impressionable unless they're clinically depressed.

Enter JOYCE.

JOYCE: I've come to say –

GERALD: Hello. Shall I take you somewhere else?

DANIEL: What did you come to say?

JOYCE: I have to go.

DANIEL: Oh.

JOYCE: I don't want to go.

DANIEL: Oh.

GERALD: Aaah.

JOYCE: I don't know what keeps me. You're hopeless and afraid.

GERALD: Aaah, aah.

DANIEL: But that's what you love…

JOYCE: Can we talk?

GERALD: Of course.

JOYCE: Not you. Not you at all.

Enter EMILY, close to tears.

EMILY: Oh Mr Roberts, Mr Daniel, and Joyce isn't it, yes – can you come? It's Wilf. I took him for a walk as Molly said, because it's so nice up here and the weather and everything, and he's been taken bad.

DANIEL: Is he breathing?

EMILY: He can't seem to make that work. Can you come?

JOYCE: Yes, of course. I'll bring some water.

EMILY: It's this way. Oh, that Molly's going to crow something dreadful about this.

JOYCE: We can use your car, Mr Roberts. I'm sure you parked nearby with Daniel's mother.

The two women go of with a bottle of water.

DANIEL: I never thought of my mother as someone in the back seat of a car.

GERALD: She wasn't.

Enter RODERICK.

RODERICK: There's somebody in trouble.

GERALD: We're coming.

RODERICK: Ariadne's with him.

GERALD: I'll take some food.

Goes off with something.

RODERICK: I think it's Emily's – er –

DANIEL: Yes. She was almost crying. (*He leaves.*)

The sound of a propeller driven aircraft has been coming over. RODERICK looks up.

RODERICK: (*To audience.*) It reminds you of the First World War flying aces, von Richthofen and people in Sopwith Pups, Knights of the Sky. Awful, of course, the airmen too terrified to speak – makes you feel – well, it takes you back. Oh, the family picnic basket.

He picks up something from it and munches and the lights fade as he reads the piece of paper with the poem on it.

Shakespeare? Copperplate?

End of Act One

ACT TWO

Scene 1

The garden. EMILY revealed wearing a hat and shaking her duster. Stops. She speaks to the audience.

EMILY: I'm still here, and the young ones are still here, but Wilf – (*Lip quivers.*) It was the pollen carried him off. He was rigid when we reached the cottage hospital, and it's left a wound as big as a melon.

Enter DANIEL with a book.

DANIEL: Ah, Emily.

EMILY: (*Shaking duster.*) Don't mind me.

DANIEL: I'm sort of sorry about Wilf, Emily.

EMILY: It's not funny.

DANIEL: I do understand and I'm really very sorry about him, though I never met him.

EMILY: Thank you.

DANIEL: It's quite hard for me to be sorry usually, but I am trying hard to be sorry now, so I'm making progress.

EMILY: Are you staying for the funeral?

DANIEL: Mother has an audition in London.

EMILY: She's never on the telly, is she.

DANIEL: She's an amateur.

EMILY: Well, don't mind me. Get on with your books.

DANIEL: Molly said – never mind.

EMILY: About an exhumation?

DANIEL: Of your mother, about whose death I wasn't sorry but am trying to be now. I expect the exhumation was one of Molly's jokes, because she can't be serious.

EMILY: I'll go and do me brasses.

DANIEL: You've got your hat on.

EMILY: It doesn't seem safe to take it off with life being so uncertain.

DANIEL: Oh it is uncertain, Emily, it is, it is.

EMILY: It is, it is.

DANIEL: It is.

EMILY: Are you all right?

DANIEL: No. No.

Enter ARIADNE.

ARIADNE: Oh Emily, you needn't have come today of all days. Why not take your hat off?

EMILY: No, thank you.

ARIADNE: We are so sad about Wilf, though with those lungs Molly did think he might have overdone things.

EMILY: What things?

DANIEL: She didn't say.

ARIADNE: She did. She told us all last night that in the potting shed –

DANIEL: No, she didn't.

ARIADNE: Yes, she did.

DANIEL: Mother, that's private.

ARIADNE: Oh! I hadn't thought.

EMILY: I'll kill that Molly.

ARIADNE: No, don't do that. She didn't say a thing, did she, Danny. Shake your duster. Do your brasses.

EMILY: And me hoovering?

ARIADNE: Of course. You're one of us.

EMILY: Has Mr Toby bought Mr Roberts' bit of garden?

ARIADNE: I think maybe he hasn't.

DANIEL: Really? Gerald told me an hour ago he thought he'd let it go, because something hadn't happened that would've stopped him.

ARIADNE: It did. It happened right here in the early morning dew.

DANIEL: You mean –

EMILY: Dew?

ARIADNE: I'm saving your grandfather's life, and I don't like doing it.

DANIEL: You slut.

EMILY: Pardon?

DANIEL: I'm speaking to my mother. That's the second time – you clearly can't control yourself.

ARIADNE: I'm trapped, Daniel, and I'm not happy about it.

EMILY: Mr Roberts can be what we used to call a dirty beast. Takes after his father, who once came mithering me in his dressing gown with cigarette holes in it so you could see his thighs, all crumbling and funny, like Molly's I expect, the old hippo. I'll go and do me brasses and then me hoovering and then I'll spit on the kitchen floor.

ARIADNE: Yes, that'll be nice.

EMILY: It will.

Enter MOLLY.

MOLLY: Are you hoovering or aren't you?

EMILY: I'm going to do me brasses so don't mither me.

MOLLY: He's dead, Emily, so don't sulk.

EMILY: I know he's dead, so don't you tell me.

DANIEL: Molly. Sympathy.

ARIADNE: Are you growing morally superior?

DANIEL: I'm developing my feminine side. People do, especially if they have a mother who splashes in the early morning dew with a global –

ARIADNE: Then show compassion for an amateur actress who wanted rather more from life.

EMILY: Some of us were happy with what we had.

MOLLY: I should think so, with that potting shed shaking like an earth –

EMILY: Don't you say another word!

MOLLY: And then you go stealing from the picnic basket.

EMILY: What picnic basket?

MOLLY: Something's missing and I want to know where it is.

ARIADNE: I took a small swiss roll, wrapped in silver paper.

MOLLY: Those who have it will know the thing I mean and I won't mind unless it's Emily. It's for the family, is that.

EMILY: (*To audience.*) Nineteen shillings in the pound and then some.

ARIADNE: Pardon?

EMILY: I'm going to work, someone has to.

She goes.

MOLLY: (*Calling.*) There'll be questions asked about your family, disappearing like slaughtered animals.

DANIEL: Is it the poem?

ARIADNE: What poem?

MOLLY: Have you got it?

DANIEL: No.

MOLLY: Emily should get the sack, Mr Daniel.

DANIEL: Molly, don't confuse everything.

MOLLY: I'll say no more, since you're disturbed.

Begins to leave.

(*As she goes, to ARIADNE.*) He needs a mother.

ARIADNE: He's got one. Are you disturbed?

DANIEL: I've lost my girl friend, my mother turns out to be a slapper, the cook fancies me – I'm doing pretty well considering my life is growing dark. The end of the world will be simple.

ARIADNE: D'you think it's true that Emily did her mother – well – in?

DANIEL: Of course not.

ARIADNE: We live very sheltered lives, you and I. There are extremely selfish people in the world, Danny, very demanding people. I didn't realise until Gerald – no, it was the war thing, really. I marched as you know, though you didn't –

DANIEL: I was researching the book.

ARIADNE: Well suddenly I saw, that day, with two million people streaming past the Ritz, I suddenly saw – what did I see?

55

DANIEL: The difference between –

ARIADNE: The difference – I must get it right –

DANIEL: The difference between good and evil.

ARIADNE: Well, yes.

DANIEL: Right.

ARIADNE: Good.

DANIEL: Have you forgotten what it was?

ARIADNE: No, I haven't. It was this. I saw that basically the difference was thoughtlessness. There. I suddenly decided I was against the war because it was thoughtless.

DANIEL: And your dislike of Mrs Blair.

ARIADNE: So you see – do sit down, I can't talk to you standing up – it wasn't being thoughtful for others to go bombing people when the money could've been spent on schools, and dentists – things like that. Zebra crossings.

DANIEL: It wasn't thoughtful for the people we were bombing.

ARIADNE: No, of course not, no, that's obvious. No. Though – no, you're right, I hadn't taken that completely on board, because Gerald says – well you know what Gerald says. He's not a thoughtful person.

DANIEL: Is he good or evil?

ARIADNE: I knew you'd make things difficult.

DANIEL: You sleep with him so you must have some idea –

ARIADNE: Only since yesterday, in an aberration, and I do know good and evil when I see them. Good is good and evil is evil, there. What is more, I'm being very good, sleeping with Gerald, because it keeps him from selling his garden so Grandfather won't have a heart attack, thus saving grandmother from coming to live with us which she wouldn't like, so there, thoughtful as anything – don't mock me, Daniel. I'm being pro-active.

DANIEL: You're having a good old fashioned affair.

ARIADNE: I'm not. What I'm doing with Gerald is self sacrifice. That's something that's not very pleasant when you do it, but is blissfully rewarding when the anaesthetic's worn off.

DANIEL: I find you dreadfully depressing.

ARIADNE: Well, depression's your thing, isn't it. I'm uplifted by it all. I'm giving myself to Gerald like the Burghers of Calais.

Enter TOBY with a small weeding hand fork.

TOBY: And what did they do? No, don't tell me, there's enough to understand without having any more. Jane's asleep and it isn't lunch time so she might be dead, there's a lot of it about, Emily's Wilf and everything, and Molly's going to exhume the mother. What'll I do with the house?

ARIADNE: Go in and see if Grandma's all right, Daniel.

TOBY: No, she may not be, and I couldn't bear it if she wasn't. The next thing is Wilf's funeral, and then Molly says give Emily the sack to cut down on expenses so I can afford another gardener which I don't want. Why've I come out here? Oh yes, so as not to find Jane dead. She never is, of course. Well?

DANIEL: Well what?

TOBY: Did you know Molly has fantasies about you?

DANIEL: I don't exactly know it.

ARIADNE: It's very sad.

TOBY: Do you have them about her?

DANIEL: Christ no. She's just always there, like a gravestone.

ARIADNE: You're a bit like her, Daniel.

DANIEL: Me?

TOBY: Well, something's up with her, she's late with the peas. Where can I dig?

Enter GERALD carrying his lap-top and speaking into a mobile phone.

GERALD: Well, offer them some more.

DANIEL: I'm not a gravestone, I'm not.

ARIADNE: Ah, Gerald.

GERALD: (*To her.*) Just a minute.

TOBY: (*Of the fork.*) This is for your garden. I'm just testing it…

He goes off.

DANIEL: I am not a gravestone.

ARIADNE: Gerald, you have told Daniel a lie about this morning and not selling the garden.

DANIEL: Mother.

GERALD: (*To phone.*) Another two hundred grand. I'll just log on to check the market.

He sits and opens his lap top.

ARIADNE: Did you hear?

GERALD: I'm waiting for someone.

ARIADNE: Who?

DANIEL: Joyce, I suppose.

TOBY re-enters brandishing a small piece of grass.

TOBY: A weed, a weed!

ARIADNE: Never mind Joyce. Let me remind you that this lawn, dew-spattered and cold, witnessed the sealing of a pact this morning, a pact not to sell your bit of garden to my father-in-law because he's not capable of looking after it.

TOBY: I *am* capable of looking after it. Look! (*Holds up weed.*) And I do not want to be saved from my own old age. I want that garden. (*He points off towards it.*)

GERALD: I haven't made up my mind about it.

DANIEL: You told me you had made up your mind.

GERALD: This morning wasn't quite such fun as yesterday, so I thought I'd ginger things up by putting about the rumour I might sell.

TOBY: For heaven's sake, it's all quite simple! Name your price and if you don't like my offer, stop fucking me about.

ARIADNE: Grandfather!

DANIEL: So apt.

TOBY: I don't know what anybody means, but I want that garden, and I've bought this fork to dig it over with. I'll stick it into someone if you don't tell me straight that I can have it.

GERALD: (*At lap top.*) Damn. Tesco's have got interested.

TOBY: In your garden?

DANIEL: No, in his super–

TOBY: Don't tell me! I'm drenched in information and none of it makes sense. What did you do on this lawn before breakfast with Gerald Roberts? No, don't say.

Enter JOYCE with knapsack which she outs down.

JOYCE: Emily's had trouble with the vacuum cleaner.

TOBY: Oh God.

DANIEL: Don't leave us.

GERALD: I thought you were going to hang around.

JOYCE: No. I'm going now, so who do I thank for whatever it is I've had?

DANIEL: It's all so sad.

GERALD: You don't have to go.

TOBY: Oh, that Roberts with the whiff of wolf about him. You can smell him loping down the lanes in the moonlight.

DANIEL: Stay. Please stay.

JOYCE: No.

DANIEL: I'm becoming sympathetic.

GERALD: You can stay next door at my place if you like, free to come and go.

ARIADNE: No, she can't. It's been lovely having her to stay, but now it's goodbye.

DANIEL: It's nothing to do with you.

ARIADNE: I fear it is.

GERALD: You're not really going to India, I hope.

DANIEL: India?

JOYCE: Since my training's over I thought I'd find a volunteer job.

DANIEL: What on earth can you do in India?

ARIADNE: Tamper with the natives?

JOYCE: I can be with them as they die.

DANIEL: Be with me instead. I'm so afraid without you, and you do like that.

JOYCE: No.

DANIEL: Please.

GERALD: She said no.

ARIADNE: And it solves the problem of who eats where at lunch.

TOBY: She'll be back to help me dig. She used to visit Jane and me when she was a little girl.

GERALD: I never knew that.

TOBY: Just as well. You go love, and leave us all to get on with things.

GERALD: You know how to reach me if you need me.

DANIEL: Are you pregnant?

ARIADNE: What?

GERALD: What?

JOYCE: That's irrelevant.

ARIADNE: It can't be. Someone will have to face it.

DANIEL: Are you?

JOYCE: It doesn't matter.

DANIEL: You're always saying things don't matter. It's middle class denial.

JOYCE: It's you who's in denial.

Enter RODERICK.

RODERICK: Something seems to be the matter with mother – grandma – Jane. Emily ran the hoover awfully near her and she woke up all distressed. She's all right, I think, but if someone could come –

TOBY: Oh, oh, she can't bear noise. I'll come. Mind out. Silly woman.

RODERICK: Which one?

TOBY exits with RODERICK.

TOBY: (*Calling.*) And you Ariadne, we need a woman's touch.

ARIADNE: I expect there'll be a bus to somewhere, but if there isn't you could always walk, couldn't you.

She goes.

DANIEL: I suppose I'm broken hearted.

JOYCE: Your mother needs you, Daniel.

He leaves.

GERALD: Well?

JOYCE: Well what?

GERALD: That's them settled. You do mean the pregnancy's irrelevant.

JOYCE: It has nothing to do with you, even if it exists.

GERALD: Well, it's something to discuss.

Enter MOLLY.

MOLLY: You've never split up from Master Daniel.

JOYCE: Yes.

MOLLY: Didn't you read – you know?

JOYCE: It was a lovely thought but I may go abroad.

MOLLY: Stay here. I'll take your bag.

JOYCE: No.

MOLLY: (*Grabbing it.*) Let me.

JOYCE: No.

MOLLY: He's a lovely boy is Daniel. (*No response.*) He's a lovely, lovely, lovely boy. (*No response.*) I'll get the peas, then. Why've they all gone in?

GERALD: Mrs Toby's in a bad way.

MOLLY: She's always pretending to die, stupid woman. (*To JOYCE.*) Don't you break my heart, miss.

She goes.

JOYCE: So it is goodbye.

GERALD: Really?

JOYCE: (*She looks out in the direction of GERALD's garden.*) Ariadne says your flower beds are always full of utterly gorgeous blooms and the lawn is absolutely immaculate. She says the whole place blossoms perfectly at every season on the dot, January to December. Who keeps it up?

GERALD: (*At his lap top.*) A gardener chappie who knows about things. He'd do it for Toby, too, if the old fool asked. Toby has a chappie of his own, of course, it's all a silly fuss about him having a heart attack, but it's getting me a bit of fun at the moment.

JOYCE: Why did you support the war?

GERALD: Gardening's a form of war. Men against weeds.

JOYCE: (*Silence.*)

GERALD: Are you going to be sincere and passionate?

JOYCE: The war was wrong.

GERALD: The war was right, and very much in this country's interests. Iraq is a dusty backward place where people die, and which needs capital investment to bring its inhabitants back to life. It also has oil to keep the engines of western industry running, so they can help a bit to modernize the place, what's left of it. It was pretty well ruined by an inefficient dictator who had to go – they all do, because all dictators are inefficient – Germany, Russia, China –

JOYCE: D'you think it's efficient to bomb it to bits? Kill its citizens, grab its oil? (*GERALD chuckles.*) It doesn't strike me as efficient to get yourself hated.

GERALD: (*Still at laptop.*) At last. Here comes the little Tiger Shops combine, can't resist the offer. (*Taps away.*) Laos will love me, you'll see. I buy up supermarkets, you know –

JOYCE: You told me on the way to the hospital. You explained how you put local farmers into the protection of the multinationals, producing cash crops at your dictated prices, that you increase global poverty by stamping on local markets –

GERALD: Oh, *The Guardian.*

JOYCE: And you never listen to anyone but yourself.

GERALD: Of course not, I'm successful. Tell me, what do you think of firms that pay sweat shop wages in the far east so that vacuum cleaners and computers – whatever – can flood into the British midlands at prices many people – most people – can afford? Prices that British wages would double if the factories were actually *in* the British midlands?

JOYCE: I think very badly of them.

GERALD: Exactly. And for the poor workers who slave to make our western lives so charming, some relief is necessary as they struggle home from sewing jeans in leaky lofts. What I'm doing is introducing them to a wholly benevolent revolution; the once a week visit to the supermarket. It leads to full fridges, easier lives, better living altogether. I'm doing good.

JOYCE: That's simply adding a cheap materialist way of life to –

GERALD: You *are* sincere. What a pity, you could've learnt something.

JOYCE: What?

GERALD: If I introduce the South East Asians to western culture, that is high quality consumer goods – ready made lasagnes are better than little bowls of undernourished rice beefed up with a hen's foot – then there will be upward pressure on wages which will have to be met and society will change, become what we call free, for all I know democratic, rich in choice, people choosing one sort of freezer over another. That's doing good, Joyce. It happens, of course, that I'll be a multi-millionaire as a result, since I make the freezers and own the supermarkets, but that's life. (*Seeing the laptop change.*) Ah! Bingo! The rice market. I'm very powerful and you like that.

JOYCE: You're very simple and that's dangerous.

GERALD: Dangerous is fun.

JOYCE: I get picked up and whisked around occasionally, and powerful men are all the same. They don't have to decide what they want because they can always have it. That makes them pretty dull.

GERALD: Make love to me.

JOYCE: Don't you have friends for that?

GERALD: I'm too busy slurping up experiences to have friends. Make love to me.

JOYCE: Like a call girl.

GERALD: If you like.

JOYCE: Powerful men are just customers, aren't they…

GERALD: I do high quality sex.

JOYCE: That makes you the call girl.

GERALD: I've explained, I'm busy.

JOYCE: I think I'll go and say goodbye to the others. It's not been very nice meeting you.

GERALD: You'll be back.

JOYCE: Oh.

Enter ARIADNE, MOLLY with peas, and TOBY.

ARIADNE: It wasn't Emily's fault.

TOBY: Thank God it was only the hoover and not the mowing machine.

MOLLY: Emily's like having Dr Shipman in the house.

TOBY: Get on with your peas.

ARIADNE: (*To JOYCE.*) You're still here.

JOYCE: I'm off now…

ARIADNE: Good. Gerald, go back to your own garden and stop seducing people.

MOLLY: We'll none of us live to enjoy that garden with Emily around.

ARIADNE: Molly?

MOLLY: (*Shelling peas with increasing viciousness.*) There really were weapons of mass destruction in that desert, you know. Them Iraqis would do anything, you can tell by their noses and their dirty moustaches and their funny churches.

JOYCE: What are you talking about?

MOLLY: That Saddam Hussein had weapons of mass

destruction because he knew he was going to get the chop – kept losing wars against the Persians, naturally – so he wanted to keep his Iraqis nice and safe from everyone – Americans, all those people – so he'd have to have something to do it with, like weapons of mass destruction. We would and all, well we do, don't we. Don't want nobody attacking us and telling us what to do, like the Russians.

ARIADNE: They're our friends now.

MOLLY: Maybe, but there's Africans and all them others, Iraqis, Saudis, Turks, Mexicans, Argentinians, they all want us, don't they. After our Queen, all of them, and the princes and the little dogs. They'll come at us like anything one day, so we have to have those weapons to get rid of them before they do. And I expect we have them all over Norfolk, Cornwall, Yorkshire, Wales.

JOYCE: I'm off. (*But stops.*)

MOLLY: It's the dole, isn't it, and the National Health. Them Arabs want to get their hands on that. They all do, take us for a soft touch, with their filthy postcards.

GERALD: Yes.

MOLLY: Well, we never were a soft touch, we fought in the trenches, my uncles died there, and then we had the Battle of Britain. You see, them Germans'll be wanting a bit before long, bloody Krauts, and the Frogs and the Wops. And the Israelis and the Palestinians. *And* there's Sweden.

ARIADNE: Sweden?

MOLLY: Of course there were weapons of mass destruction. And there's Emily left out there with Mrs Toby. She's a weapon of mass destruction and no mistake – her mother, her paramour, heaven knows who else.

TOBY: I've never heard you say things like this before.

MOLLY: You haven't been listening, have you. There's Mrs Roderick dithering away and going on marches, makes me sick. And Master Daniel writing a book and I've never seen him touch a pen. And even Mr Roberts, who has the right ideas, he wastes himself being dirty.

TOBY: You had it off with a canon of the Church of England.

GERALD: Did you?

MOLLY: There, you see. Once you could trust employers to keep a secret, but now, it's rotten, all of it. Get rid of Emily.

JOYCE: I will go now. Goodbye.

Enter RODERICK.

RODERICK: Ah. Daniel says you're as it were – um –

JOYCE: I really do have to go.

GERALD: (*Taking her by the arm.*) I'll give you a lift to a bus. You can have my garden, Toby.

ARIADNE: Gerald!

GERALD: I can show it to you on the way. My car's parked there.

JOYCE: Let go of me.

GERALD: What?

MOLLY: Remember Daniel, remember the poem, and remember me.

JOYCE: I'll certainly do that.

She leaves, followed by GERALD.

And I'll find my own way.

GERALD: You'll need a lift, so don't be naïve…

TOBY: It's like having an unexploded bomb in the kitchen

with you there. Go and cook your chops and keep out of the way.

MOLLY: I haven't finished my peas.

RODERICK: Why is there so much feeling everywhere?

TOBY: We've been talking war in here which is a change, except that Molly has been very unpleasant.

RODERICK: And the poem – Is this it?

MOLLY: Give it here. (*She folds the poem and tucks it into the top of her apron.*) We've all got to stick together, like Chuchill said.

RODERICK: I think it's Shakespeare.

MOLLY: It is Shakespeare.

RODERICK: Not Church – Oh – Yes, I see. Poor Daniel's dreadfully upset.

ARIADNE: I'll talk to him later.

MOLLY: What about?

TOBY: I've got my garden, then. I'll work away at it and if I have a stroke it'll serve you all right for being so negative. Have I mentioned the Welsh farmer today, the one who thought –

ALL: Yes.

TOBY: So that's the ration used up.

Enter DANIEL.

DANIEL: Has she gone?

ARIADNE: She's looking at the new garden with Gerald.

MOLLY: She won't like it so there's your chance. Take it.

DANIEL: Aren't we going to have anything to eat today?

TOBY: When she's done her peas and cooked her chops,

which she's being incompetent about.

MOLLY: And peeled my potatoes.

RODERICK: Well go and do that.

ADELAIDE: Roddy?

RODERICK: Well –

MOLLY: (*Getting up.*) There'll be time for you to go and argue with them and talk about the warming up of things and all that rubbish.

TOBY: Go and get our lunch before I fire you.

MOLLY: That'll be the day. (*Leaves.*)

DANIEL: I think I will go and see what's happening.

TOBY: We'll all go. Peeling takes Molly fifteen minutes, chops twenty, the peas about ten, she does them all at the same time so say twenty-five – Let's get a drink, Daniel, and go over to the new property.

DANIEL: I might cry.

TOBY and DANIEL leave.

RODERICK: Pre-lunch drinks always make me so expectant.

ARIADNE: Let's go and see how he's handling the girl, and spit on him.

They leave.

Scene 2

Enter JOYCE followed by GERALD. She has her knapsack in her hand, as she has never yet put it on over her shoulders. She is angry.

JOYCE: It's wrong. It's wrong to lie, it's wrong to kill, it's wrong to steal, it's wrong to pretend things are what they aren't, it's wrong to fight when there's another way, it's wrong to ignore agreements, it's all wrong, wrong, thronged with wrong – and wrong to drag three whole continents into a dishonest mess we all knew was going to be useless and horrible and designed to keep the balance of power among the wealthy, no matter who dies. No, listen. The world's a more dangerous place than it ever was, not just because the war was a lie from the start, but because it is always wrong to be so sure you're right that you won't stop to think. I mean, if a centre of enormous wealth is destroyed out of the blue one day, at the same time as a centre of huge military power, you'd think someone would sit down and try to work out the symbolism of that, instead of prating on about freedom, and evil and the cowardice of Muslims. That attack was all about wealth and armies. Anyone could see that. Anyone, of course, except the president. He's a child, and a foolish child and a rich child and he doesn't think what things mean. And the prime minister's the same, not thinking through the meaning of things, and so they behave like children, pushing soldiers about as if Iraq was the nursery floor, full of nursery names – Shock and Awe, Weapons of Mass Destruction, Road Map to Peace – Go Past Go and Take Two Billion Pounds –

GERALD: You're very beautiful when –

JOYCE: Don't you dare say that. There might be something about you when you're powerful and unaware, but when you're trite and hackneyed, there's nothing.

GERALD: I am trite and hackneyed. When a country is a danger to the world, and the people in it are being tortured, I think it should be bombed.

JOYCE: Who bombed? The farmers? The shopkeepers? The supermarket managers, even? They aren't a danger to the world. Corporate finance, should that be bombed? Governments with the most powerful armies and air forces, the biggest pile of nuclear bombs and the willingness to strike first in the name of personal comfort – isn't that what some people thought that day, that some of us should be bombed because we used up too much energy, piled up too many arms, and sent people to work in leaky lofts to keep us as you say in a charming way of life? And has it ever occurred to anyone in power over here to sit down and say, 'It must've meant something, that devastation in New York. It wasn't just done for fun. Not even for religion.' No. No-one has thought about it, especially not people like you who just go along with the big boys, travelling first class and burning oil without a thought of where it's going to come from. You felt helpless that day, and it was strange for you, so you wanted to hit someone, guilty or not, and call it saving civilization.

GERALD: Perhaps we could forget our differences and just make –

JOYCE: We can't. Tell me what those flowers are.

GERALD: I don't know. Those are delphiniums, I think. They look almost dead.

JOYCE: Cut them down and they'll flower again, several times, I believe.

GERALD: What about that yellow thing?

JOYCE: Sunflower. Once a season. How can you pretend the war was civilizing?

GERALD: Sadam was cruel as well as inefficient.

JOYCE: But wrong is wrong. Wrong. Even Ariadne is groping towards that as an idea, I'm told. The trouble is – the trouble is right isn't always right. Wrong is always wrong, but right – it's very difficult to do right.

GERALD: In that case, can we –

JOYCE: No.

GERALD: Actually, you wouldn't still be here if there wasn't a part of you that wanted to know what making love with me was like.

JOYCE: I'm here, transfixed, because you offend me so much. We speak quite openly to each other, and yet there's an ocean behind each of us, two oceans that can't possibly join together without – they lap at the separating wall – oh, they are dangerous.

GERALD: Are you weakening?

JOYCE: No.

Enter EMILY.

EMILY: It's only me.

GERALD: Emily.

EMILY: (*To audience.*) Not at it, you see, being so different.

JOYCE: Emily?

EMILY: I was just wanting a look at what you've given Mr Toby. Oh – it's lovely, vistas like in a seed catalogue.

GERALD: Thank you. Now, if you –

EMILY: (*Sitting.*) Wilf and me did gardening. We always wanted vistas, but of course Mother never liked what we planted. I sometimes thought Mother was a man, so many whiskers. You never knew her, I suppose.

GERALD: Perhaps my father –

EMILY: No, he knew me.

JOYCE: *Knew* you?

EMILY: But even then I knew that Wilf was my one true love, so I said 'No, thank you, Mr Roberts,' and he drew his dressing gown about him.

GERALD: You mean my father got his kit off for you?

73

EMILY: And once he fiddled with his Burberry mackintosh. That was on a wet November evening, and a bit foggy, outside the Methodist church.

GERALD: Always the Woolworth end of religion. Joyce, just come inside for a minute. I've a present for you. As a friend.

JOYCE: You can't help it, can you. It's in the genes.

EMILY: Best go in, dear. You never know when the chance'll come again and it's a lovely house. Of course, your Aunt Molly wouldn't approve, him not being Daniel.

JOYCE: I've seen houses like this.

EMILY: It's up to you, but never miss a chance to look in someone's home, because it won't come back.

JOYCE: I don't know what you mean.

GERALD: I do.

JOYCE: You're mad. I will come in to look, but I warn you, Gerald, I have a quick temper, and I'm very strong. Don't try a thing.

GERALD and JOYCE exit.

EMILY: (*To the audience.*) Well, it is true, you never know what can happen when opportunity knocks, and when you reach a certain time of life it does stop knocking. (*Grins.*) Molly will be furious.

Enter TOBY, with little fork, RODERICK, DANIEL and ARIADNE. All have drinks.

TOBY: Mine, all mine!

DANIEL: There is a lot for grandfather to care for.

TOBY: Emily?

DANIEL: But since we'll all be dead soon anyway –

ARIADNE: We won't be dead.

RODERICK: Someone'll think of something, they always do.

EMILY: It could've been mine, all this.

TOBY: Yours?

ARIADNE: One flash doesn't make a codicil, Emily.

TOBY: Where shall I start?

EMILY: The vistas are very large.

TOBY: Exactly. Here comes your new master, vistas.

He exits brandishing fork.

RODERICK: Where are Joyce and Gerald, I wonder?

EMILY: I think I must do me shopping.

ARIADNE: Where are they?

EMILY: They went into the house to get a present.

ARIADNE: You let them?

EMILY: It's not my place to stop people doing things, madam. I'm the daily help, suspected of murder. Goodbye, Mr Daniel, and thank you for nearly feeling sorry.

DANIEL: They're alone?

EMILY: Yes.

RODERICK: We're going to stay over for the funeral, Emily.

EMILY: Oh, Wilf will be pleased when I tell him.

ARIADNE: He's dead.

EMILY: So Molly says. Till tomorrow.

She exits.

ARIADNE: It's strange how you feel jealous, even if you didn't like what you're jealous about.

RODERICK: Would you like me to say something to Gerald – how tasteless it is to choose someone in preference to my wife? Especially a younger someone?

ARIADNE: Later.

DANIEL: Shall I go inside, mother?

ARIADNE: Possibly.

DANIEL: I'm asking for advice.

RODERICK: You might get hurt.

DANIEL: I almost want that. And I could hit him.

Enter TOBY, the fork bent and a bit of delphinium.

TOBY: It's harder than I thought, but I've made my mark.

RODERICK: Well done, father.

TOBY: Have I said that life is like a piece of abstract – ?

ALL: Yes.

RODERICK: Perhaps I could say something now. I've come across Ariadne in various indelicate positions over the last twenty-four hours, and my son says we're all going to die and writes a book about it, and my father wants to kill himself digging up pretty flowers, and his housekeeper accuses the daily help of murder, and I ask you, what does it all mean – what does it mean?

DANIEL: I think I will go in, mother.

ARIADNE: Yes do, your father may be some time.

DANIEL slips out.

RODERICK: The thing is, why aren't we putting it right? I mean, if the plumbing goes wrong, we call in a little man, he puts it right, we pay him and that's fine. Same with the electrics, the car, everything. Well, why can't we call in a little man to fix – well, whatever it is?

ARIADNE: Are you suggesting an increase in taxation, Roderick?

RODERICK: No, of course not, but sometimes I just feel – it doesn't matter.

TOBY: Right.

RODERICK: In the way.

ARIADNE: Oh, dear Roddy.

RODERICK: Like a hen that's stopped laying eggs, but still insists on being fed.

MOLLY: (*Off.*) Where are you all?

TOBY: Oh God, the chops are done.

MOLLY: Lunch is going cold.

TOBY: Come and see the new garden and be pleased.

MOLLY: (*Entering.*) I can't unplug the hoover.

TOBY: Have you left it near Jane?

MOLLY: You left her alone with Emily and the hoover was right next to her.

RODERICK: Has it turned on again?

MOLLY: Emily did it, not me.

Enter JOYCE wiping her hands, followed by DANIEL.

DANIEL: What were you doing in that corridor?

JOYCE: (*Smiling.*) Not much. It was like milking a cow. (*She picks up her knapsack.*) Goodbye, everyone. I won't be back

She goes.

MOLLY: Don't leave us, Joyce. Daniel, follow her.

DANIEL: I never want to see her again, not ever. She's cheap and nasty.

MOLLY: I've cared for you. (*Waves the poem.*) I've loved you all. And the hoover's switch is jammed. I don't know what to do.

TOBY: Come along Molly, let's go and see. We all make mistakes.

MOLLY: Not me. I never do. (*Nearly a sob.*)

They leave.

ARIADNE: Go with them, Daniel.

DANIEL: Treated like a child. We're all going to die, you know.

He follows.

ARIADNE: He'll do well eventually, Roddy.

RODERICK: No. No, he won't. Do you remember history lessons at school? There was always a bit called The Rise of The Merchant Class. It was always happening, The Rise of the Merchant Class, about twice a century, The Rise of the Merchant Class, followed by a religious war, and then it happened again, The Rise of the Merchant Class, a kind of chorus, sensible, boring, well to do, and plump. And here we are again, the Merchant Class, still rising, like a half open umbrella in a drain pipe, not letting anything get past, blocking all movement except our own. Dreadful. I think Daniel will to drift into that.

ARIADNE: Perhaps this time it'll fade away.

RODERICK: Such things only happen in stories about nineteenth century Russia.

ARIADNE: There must be some alternative to us.

RODERICK: There are always more possibilities than

there are alternatives.

Sound of old aeroplane again.

ARIADNE: (*Looking up.*) There's one of your favourite aeroplanes.

RODERICK: (*Not looking anywhere.*) Let's go and see what Molly's done.

ARIADNE: Yes. (*She leaves. He stays where he is. Aeroplane still sounds.*)

RODERICK: So – heigh ho. (*Thoughtful pause.*). Heigh fucking ho. (*Thoughtful pause.*) Heigh fuck, fuck, fuck, fuck, fuck…

Lights fade on the repetition of this word.

The End.

By the same author

David Cregan: Three Plays
Whispers Along the Patio / Nice Dorothy / The Last Thrash
9781840022452

WWW.OBERONBOOKS.COM

Follow us on www.twitter.com/@oberonbooks
& www.facebook.com/OberonBooksLondon